S0-AVG-842

Smart Soapmaking
The Simple Guide to Making Traditional Handmade Soap Quickly, Safely, and Reliably

— Anne L. Watson —

Maybe you've made melt-and-pour soap and want to move on to something more challenging and rewarding. Maybe traditional soapmaking appeals to you, but you figure it's too difficult or dangerous. Or maybe you're already doing it, but outmoded ideas and methods are complicating the process and slowing you down.

No matter which of these fits you, you'll find *Smart Soapmaking* practical, helpful, and refreshing. Written by a former professional soapmaker, this book explodes the myths about soapmaking and shows you how to make luxurious soap with the least fuss and bother.

"Should become *the* book for soapmaking. . . . It's about time someone wrote a book like this. Most are idealistic and inaccurate. This book has a wonderful common sense approach that is SO long overdue. . . . I can recommend it with 100% confidence."

Susan Kennedy, Oregon Trail Soaps
Rogue River, Oregon

"Smart it is . . . . A simple, no-nonsense book that cuts through the curmudgery of stifling soap bibles like no other."

Shellie Humphries
Harstine Island, Washington

"A great book for beginners, with clear and easy instructions."

Anne-Marie Faiola, Bramble Berry Inc.
Bellingham, Washington

"I learned more from *Smart Soapmaking* than from any other soaping book, and I have read quite a few. . . . It's written with the average person in mind, not a chemistry major. Directions are very simple and easy to understand. It really takes the mystery out of making soap."

Jackie Pack
Stuart, Virginia

"Written in an easy, casual style that reminded me of an in-person soapmaking class. The information is practical, helpful, and easy to understand."

Barb Miller, Miller's Homemade Soaps
Westfield, Pennsylvania

"Excellent . . . . The simplicity and fear quashing is wonderfully reassuring to the beginning soaper."

Kerry Pearson, Heirloom Body Care
Llandilo, New South Wales

"The directions are more practical than in other soapmaking books I've read. I was also happy to see how many great sources for materials and information the book provided. The book will save soapmakers a lot of time and effort."

Pamela Paine, Butternut Creek Farm Soaps
Dorset, Ohio

"Written with a delightful voice and humor."

Kathy Miller, Miller's Homemade Soap Pages
Silverdale, Washington

"I wish Smart Soapmaking had been my first book on soap. It simplifies the process, and it just makes sense. . . . Covers several months worth of questions."

Phyllis Driggs
Liberty, Indiana

"Excellent . . . . Easy to read, practical, down to earth. Performs the greatly needed service of dispelling myths, which it does with a sense of humor."

Loretta Liefveld, Nature's Wild Child
Rancho Cucamonga, California

"A necessity for those just starting out who want to do it right from the very first time."

Megan Baillie
Budd Lake, New Jersey

"BRILLIANT to find the recipes are in grams as well as ounces."

Jude Birch, Aussie Soap Supplies
Bicton, West Australia

"Way overdue. . . . A gift of common sense caution, proven methods, tried-and-true shortcuts, and some excellent recipes as well, for both the professional/experienced soapmaker and the eager beginner."

Deb Petersen, Shepherd's Soap Co.
Shelton, Washington

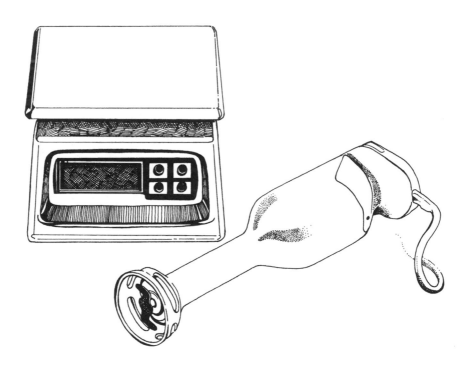

Smart Soapmaking

The Simple Guide to Making
Traditional Handmade Soap
Quickly, Safely, and Reliably

Anne L. Watson

Illustrated by Wendy Edelson

Shepard Publications
Olympia, Washington

Author Online!

For updates and more resources,
visit Anne's Soapmaking Page at

www.annelwatson.com/soapmaking

Text copyright © 2007 by Anne L. Watson
Illustrations copyright © 2007 by Shepard Publications
All rights reserved. Permission is granted to copy or reprint
portions for any noncommercial use, except they may not be
posted online without permission.

ISBN 978-0-938497-42-4

Library of Congress Control Number: 2006931059
Library of Congress subject heading: Soap

Version 1.1

For Aaron

Contents

Acknowledgments

Since I didn't invent the craft of soapmaking, I'm indebted to more individuals than I can count, going back millennia.

More directly, I've learned from books and Web sites, especially those mentioned in the resources section in the back of this book; from uncountable members of Internet mailing lists, whose advice can only be honored by "paying it forward;" and from the people who reviewed and tried out early versions of the book and gave dozens of helpful suggestions.

Special thanks to Connie Rutter, who gave me a chemist's views on soapmaking. To Kathy Ford of AOK Soaps, who showed me how to make soap when I was scared to try. To Kathy Miller of Miller's Homemade Soap Pages, Susan Kennedy of Oregon Trail Soaps, and a number of others for last-minute testing of my idea of using a thermometer to gauge the readiness of a soap mixture. And especially to my husband, Aaron Shepard, who edited, designed, and published this book.

A Few First Thoughts

"Make soap when the moon is waning, or it will be harsh."

"You have to stir soap clockwise, or it won't set."

"Soap has to be stirred with a sassafras stick."

You probably wouldn't believe any of these old superstitions. But soapmaking instructions today can be almost as illogical. They make the process seem complicated and difficult. They make it look terribly dangerous.

It isn't.

Maybe you're like some of my students. Until they took my class, they were afraid to try soapmaking. I love it when the class is finished and they say, "Well, of all things—is *that* all there is to it?"

Or maybe you've made soap, but you wonder if everything you learned to do is really necessary. If there's a simpler way, you'd sure like to know.

In either case, I've been in your shoes. I started out afraid to try soapmaking, and then a friend taught me how. But for a long time I believed a lot of old wives' tales about it. I did some things that now seem as silly to me as any of the superstitions I quote above.

When I began to suspect that some of what I'd learned was nonsense, I decided to find out what was true and what wasn't. So I started asking people, and nagging people, and trading soap for technical information. I barged around the

Internet and bugged librarians and teachers. I studied soap-making books, watched a video, and even learned computer programs, all to see what different people had to say about the things I wanted to know. Good thing I'm a grownup—if I were a kid, people would have told me I was a pest. As it was, they probably just thought it.

When I couldn't get answers any other way, I experimented on my own. *What will happen if I don't follow this rule?* Sometimes, nothing. *Bye-bye, rule.* More often, though, I found that techniques useful for babying particular recipes had been cast as rules to apply to all. In this book, I tell you when you're likely to need such techniques and when you can skip them.

One of the main things that I learned was to not blindly accept what I was told. Short of sticking my finger into a lye solution to see if it really would burn me—and don't you do that, either—I tested nearly everything. So, unlike some soap-making books, this one isn't based on handed-down information. It's based on things I've tried. Once in a while, I do accept someone's word for something, but when I do, I've been careful to say so.

On the other hand, I'm not equipped to run a testing lab. I'm certain of my results for the recipes and batch sizes I've worked with. Other ingredients or quantities may give different results. So, "go by the book" at first, then experiment further if you like.

Or skip the experimenting and just make soap.

Superstitions Galore!
Myths about Soap and Soapmaking

There are a great many misconceptions about soapmaking. Let's take time to dispel some of them, starting with a few that make people afraid to make soap.

Myths That Scare You Away

Myth #1: Soapmaking is difficult.

"I stirred that pot for two days, and I never did get it to make soap."

When I was fairly new to making soap, I joined a couple of Internet mailing lists for soapmakers. The messages included lots of "Help!" emails from people who had been stirring a batch for hours or days and couldn't make it work.

I wondered how they did it. How do you get a batch of soap to fail? I couldn't think of a polite way to ask.

Years later, I posed this question to a group of experienced soapmakers. They agreed that by far the most common cause of "Help!" emails is that new soapmakers try to design their own recipes before they know how. Making soap and designing recipes are two different crafts. It's best to learn them one at a time. So start with recipes that are tried and true.

Some of those writers of "Help!" messages may have unknowingly picked difficult recipes. A theme you'll find over and over in this book is that different soap recipes vary dramatically in what it takes to make them. Some are easy and some aren't.

And just because a recipe is harder doesn't mean the soap it makes is better. I'll show you how to figure that out in advance.

Myth #2: Soapmaking is expensive.

"You need all this special equipment, and the ingredients cost a lot too."

We're not setting up a factory here. Aside from a couple of special items, soapmaking uses more or less the same tools that cooking does. Many soapmakers use their regular kitchen equipment, and do it safely. Yes, you're using lye, but lye isn't plutonium. It's easily neutralized, diluted, and removed. If you wash your equipment carefully, there's no reason not to use your kitchenware. "Carefully" is the key word here—you don't want soap in the soup, or soup in the soap.

But the idea still bothers some people. And some materials, such as aluminum, tin, and copper, work fine for cookware, but you can't use them in soapmaking because they react with lye. So you may not want or even be able to use some things from your kitchen.

If you buy pots, look for stainless or enameled steel. Enameled steel spatterware is usually inexpensive. Restaurant supply stores often have great prices on stainless steel pots.

Your other tools and containers may be stainless steel, enameled steel, heat-resistant plastic, or oven-safe glass. Chances are, you have plenty of usable stuff in your cabinets and drawers. If you're not sure a plastic container is heat-resistant, fill it with boiling water. If you decide to buy equipment, shop around—best of all, visit a thrift store (charity shop, in the U.K.), discount store, or dollar store.

As to materials, you can make soap from just about any fat—anything from the cheapest vegetable oil or shortening in the grocery store to the most exotic, unpronounceable substance ever wrung from a tropical plant. Some of the best materials are the ones that are plentiful and cheap. Don't think ingredients are better just because they cost more.

A final point on expense: If you can make good soap, you can make it for gifts—beautiful, greatly-appreciated gifts. And for almost all of us, that's less expensive than hitting the malls for every event that comes along. Any money you invest should come back to you from that alone.

Myth #3: Handmade soap is harsh.

"Oh, lye soap. . . . It's rough on your skin, isn't it? I don't want to make that."

Most of us have heard about homemade country soap that would "take your hide right off." But country soap wasn't harsh *because* it was made with lye. *All* soap is made with lye, even the glycerin soap blocks sold in craft stores. Even luxury soaps that sell for more than most of us would pay.

Country soap was harsh because the quality of ingredients was unreliable and there was a lot the soapmakers didn't know. They rendered their own fats and made their own lye from hardwood ashes and rainwater. They had no test for the strength of their lye solution other than floating an egg in it. Their recipes were hit-and-miss.

Today, most soapmakers buy their fats and lye already prepared. They work from precise formulations that carefully balance the ingredients. In finished soap that's made properly, no lye remains.

So how do you make it properly?

To begin with, use the recipes and directions in this book. Before we're done, I'll show you how to check a soap recipe you find elsewhere, as well as how to design your own.

Myth #4: Soapmaking is dangerous.

"Well, I don't want to mess around with lye."

I don't know why, but nearly everyone says *"mess* around with lye," as if soapmaking involved slinging the stuff all over the place. I assure you, it doesn't. You stir some lye into water, and mix the lye solution with fat. I have yet to make a mess doing that. And I have yet to get burned.

Of course, you *can*. If you're careless with lye, you may well get hurt. If you're careless riding a bicycle, you may get hurt too. This doesn't keep many people from riding bicycles. It just makes them take reasonable care when they ride. They wear protective gear and pay attention to what they're doing.

That strategy works in soapmaking too. Your protective gear for soapmaking is goggles and gloves, and you wear them whenever you work with lye.

Like when you're mowing the lawn, keep pets and children away from where you're working. Like household cleaners, soapmaking ingredients must be stored safely. Label everything, whether you think it's hazardous or not. Keep all containers closed tightly and out of reach of children and pets.

Like driving a car, soapmaking should be avoided when you're feeling impaired in any way—tired, angry, tipsy, distracted, sick, rushed, whatever. Like frying in deep fat, soapmaking needs your full attention. Once you've mixed the lye solution, stick strictly to what you're doing till your soap is finished. Don't leave the lye unattended, even for "just a minute"—especially if you have pets or kids. Using my methods, this won't be a problem, because you won't need the long cooling times you would with most other instructions.

We all do things each day that require care. So, when you make soap, just be careful—you already know how.

Myths That Lead You Astray

So far, I've discussed myths that are believed by people who haven't made soap. But there's another whole class of misconceptions held by soapmakers themselves.

Some of these ideas—like needing to stir with a sassafras stick—must be centuries old. Not many people would still believe that. But some myths are offered as truth by half the soapmaking books today and a similar percentage of Web sites.

Remember the joke about the guy who snaps his fingers to keep elephants away? His friend says, "But there's no elephants around here." And the guy says, "Yeah, it works, don't it?"

Some soapmaking instructions are like that. If you take a lot of time and trouble to do what they say, the recipe works. But it works just as well if you don't. So, why bother?

Here are a few misconceptions and mystifications still making the rounds.

Myth #5: You have to mix soap till you get trace.

One thing that puzzles new soapmakers is instructions to stir your soap mixture till it shows a condition called *trace*. This is described as when the mixture is so thick that, if you dribble a bit of the mixture back into the pot, a "trace" of what you dribble will remain on the surface.

Beginning soapmaking books often contain close-up photos of soap at trace. I remember squinting at many of them, trying to figure it all out. When I started making soap, I made two successful batches, fretting about trace the whole time. The soap came out fine, but I was sure I was doing something wrong. I hadn't seen anything that looked like the photos.

It was my good luck to have a friend who had been a high school chemistry teacher. When I phoned and told her about my difficulties with trace, she asked what it was. I was surprised a chemist didn't know, but I explained as best I could.

There was a brief silence. Of course I couldn't see her, but she was probably rubbing her forehead—which she does when anyone says something that makes no sense.

Finally, she said, "You don't need to worry about that. If you just measure correctly, control the temperature, and mix your ingredients well, you'll get soap."

I decided to follow her advice, and I've never lost a batch of soap. Follow mine, and you won't either.

But why the difference? Are all those soap books wrong?

Not really. With hand stirring, you *do* have to look for trace. That's because *saponification*—the chemical reaction that creates soap—has to thicken the mixture to that point before you can stop stirring and pour it into the mold. Otherwise, some of the fat and the lye solution could still separate, leaving the reaction incomplete.

But in modern craft soapmaking, hand stirring is most often replaced by use of a stick blender. This blends the fat and the lye solution so rapidly and thoroughly that they quickly get mixed down to a microscopic level. That not only gets the mixture saponifying a whole lot faster, it also helps hold the fat and the lye solution together while it's happening.

Of course, the chemistry is more complicated than that, but the bottom line is that you don't have to wait for the mixture to thicken all the way to trace before pouring it into the mold. It will get there *after* you pour it.

How do you know when you can stop blending? Don't worry, I'll describe the signs for you. You'll be able to tell by sight, by sound, and even by temperature. Yes, you'll be able to gauge it with a thermometer!

Once again, recipes vary. For a few temperamental ones, you *may* need to let the mixture come fully to trace before pouring it out. But for most recipes—including any of the ones in this book—you don't.

Myth #6: The lye solution and the fat must be at the same temperature.

One of the oldest and most common errors in soapmaking craft books is to say that these ingredients must be at exactly the same temperature before you mix them. It seems that one of the first such books was written by someone who believed it, and it's been passed down ever since. You still come across complicated instructions for using hot and cold water baths to match the temperatures—instructions that would keep a barrel of monkeys busy.

It's just not true. There's a range of about twenty degrees Fahrenheit (eleven degrees Celsius) that's perfect for soapmaking. You'll do fine when your lye solution and your fat are each anywhere in this range—and I make it easy to get them there.

Myth #7: Soap must be incubated.

Another fallacy is that soap must be kept warm after it's poured into the mold. All sorts of little nests and incubators have been prescribed for this purpose. Some soap books give dire warnings that the soap won't set if you even *peek* at it while it's getting there.

According to this myth, soap has to go through a "gel stage." Now, it's true that soap becomes a kind of gel if you hold in the heat. Then, as it cools, it becomes solid and opaque—just like soap that *hasn't* gone through a "gel stage."

Temperature during the setting period has little or nothing to do with soap setting. I've tried to make soap fail by pouring it into molds that don't conserve heat and then putting them in a cold place. No matter what I did, the soap came out fine. In fact, when I asked other soapmakers about this, I learned that most milk soap mixtures are actually *cooled*. If a soap mixture *doesn't* set, the reason is usually excess water in the recipe—*not* temperature.

In some cases, though, warming may have other advantages. Some recipes produce soap with a sort of thin rind if the mixture isn't kept warm. This rind doesn't hurt anything, and you can trim it off—but warming may prevent it entirely.

Also, some soapmakers report that warming creates a better texture in soap from the recipes they use. Others say warming makes the texture worse! In my own testing, I've noticed no difference at all. In any case, you will certainly get soap, whether you warm it or not.

Myth #8: Soap takes many weeks to stop being caustic—or it takes no time at all.

Many soapmakers believe soap is caustic for more than a month after you make it. That's the older myth. The newer, opposite one is that soap should be completely usable within hours. A few soapmakers take this to extremes—if soap isn't ready for use as soon as it's solid, they say it was made with too much lye.

In my experience, neither of these notions is true. I've experimented with quite a few soap recipes, testing the soap with pH strips and by using it. The results depended on the recipe. Almost all soaps I tried could be used on my hands right out of the mold—but using some of the same ones on my face convinced me they do become milder over as much as two weeks.

But apart from that, new soap can get mushy fast if you use it before it has a chance to dry out a little. So, regardless of mildness, it's good to store the soap in a well-ventilated area for at least a couple of weeks.

*　*　*

Once again, don't believe everything you hear or read. Even books have errors—and if you swallow everything you see on the Internet, you may wind up stirring your soap clockwise with a sassafras stick under a waning moon.

What Is Soap, Anyway?
What It Is and What Goes Into It

First of all, here's what soap isn't: It probably isn't the stuff you buy in the supermarket. Most bar "soap" is actually solid detergent. Check the labeling on the wrapper. You almost never see the word "soap."

So, what is soap?

Soap is formed by combining fat with lye. The soap is produced by a chemical reaction between them, called *saponification*. A bit of trivia: Chemically, soap is a salt.

Traditionally, the mixture of fat and lye was boiled. But today the most common technique for making soap by hand is *cold process,* or CP, the method discussed in this book. (By the way, "cold process" doesn't mean that everything stays cool, but only that you don't add heat yourself once the ingredients are mixed.) Other soapmaking methods include *melt and pour* (MP), *hot process* (HP), *cold process oven process* (CPOP, pronounced "SEE-pop"), and *rebatching*.

The soap from all these methods comes from fat and lye, though for some methods they're already combined for you. Other ingredients include water or a water-based liquid to dissolve the lye, and optional additives like colorant and scent.

To get the results you want, you need to know a little about soapmaking ingredients. Let's take a closer look at the different kinds.

Fat

Soapmaking fat comes from both animal and plant sources. Mineral oils cannot be used to make soap.

Soapmakers classify fats by whether they're liquid or solid at room temperature. Generally, the liquid fats are called "oils," and the solid fats are called "butters." But the use of these terms can vary. Some solid fats, such as lard and tallow, aren't called butters. Some "oils" are actually solid fats—palm oil, for example.

The most confusing case is coconut oil, with its melting point around 76°F (or around 25°C). This means it's usually solid but can become liquid in the heat of summer. To add to the confusion, a partially hydrogenated form of coconut oil is solid to 92°F (about 33°C), while a form called *fractionated* is liquid at all normal temperatures.

To make the confusion of terms complete, many soapmakers simply don't like the term *fat*—often because they equate it only to animal fats like lard and tallow—so they refer to *all* other fats as "oils." Of course, you can use any terms you like—but for clarity and accuracy in this book, I'll stick to the term *fat* for all these soapmaking materials, whether solid or liquid, animal or plant.

In traditional country soapmaking, the solid fats were usually a by-product of meat butchering on the farm. Fat for soap would be made by rendering beef or pork fat. Today, soapmakers get beef tallow and pork lard ready-made. But a few specialty soapmakers still render their own animal fats, which may now include such exotics as buffalo and emu.

Soapmakers differ about using animal fat. Tallow and lard make good, inexpensive soap, but if you're opposed to their use, you can choose from many excellent fats made from plants. The recipe I start you with has no animal fat.

Among soapmaking fats from plants, the solid fats include shea butter (from shea nuts), coconut oil, avocado butter, and palm oil. The liquid fats include all the cooking and salad oils, as well as shea oil (fractionated shea butter), castor oil, and the oil of numerous other seeds—from flax seed to peach pits.

One of the principal oils in soapmaking is olive oil. (In traditional Castile soap recipes, it's the one and only fat.) Any grade of olive oil will do—you don't need a grade meant for fine cooking. In fact, olive-pomace oil, the worst choice for cooking, is said to be the best for soapmaking.

Basic oils such as corn, safflower, olive, and coconut are sold by grocery stores, health food stores, food co-ops, restaurant suppliers, and big-box discount stores.

Exotic oils and almost all butters will probably have to be bought from stores that sell soapmaking supplies, or from catalogs or Internet sources. You may find just what you're looking for from a small supplier that serves a special market niche. Though catalogs and Internet sources may sell basic oils as well, and at lower prices, buying those locally may be cheaper, because you avoid shipping costs.

Lye

The other most important ingredient in soapmaking is *lye*. This name can actually refer to any of several *alkalis*—a kind of strong *base,* the opposite of an acid—and it can even refer to those alkalis plus the water they're dissolved in. But nowadays "lye" almost always just means the dry form of sodium hydroxide, or *caustic soda*—and that's what you'll use in your soapmaking. (Liquid soap, by the way, takes a different kind of lye—potassium hydroxide, or *caustic potash*.)

In the past, lye was made by leaching wood ashes. One reason that "granny soap" was often harsh was that homemade lye varied in strength. Having lye available in a standardized, industrially-produced form is one of the main reasons soapmaking today is safe and predictable. The recipes and techniques in this book assume you're using commercial lye. I definitely don't recommend making your own.

Formerly, lye was readily available in grocery stores—but in some communities it has been taken off the shelves because it's used in making not only soap but also illegal drugs. You might find it at a hardware or home improvement store (DIY store, in the U.K.). If not, chemical suppliers may sell small quantities. Or buy from soapmaking supply Web sites or from other soapmakers.

The label should say "100% lye" or "100% sodium hydroxide." Never use a drain cleaning product that doesn't state this, because the lye will be combined with other ingredients that can't be used in soapmaking.

Water

In the past, soapmakers often used rainwater for its purity. For the same reason, today's soap recipes almost always call for distilled water. You should use distilled at least for your first efforts, since minerals in tap, spring, and well water can affect your soap. After that, if you want to experiment with another kind of water, go ahead. If it doesn't work, you can always go back to distilled—or set out a rain barrel.

When I learned soapmaking, recipes had a fairly high percentage of water, and we were told to let the soap dry out for six weeks. The current trend is to minimize water so the soaps can be used sooner—but that can have its own disadvantages when you work with lye. Since the recipes in this book will be used by beginners, I've designed them with medium amounts of water.

Other liquids besides plain water can be used in soapmaking. Some soapmakers use teas made from soothing herbs such as chamomile. (Other soapmakers see no point, believing the herbs lose their desirable qualities in the process.) Making soap with milk involves special techniques not covered in this book, but you can find several books and Web sites on it if you're interested.

Additives

Probably everything but the cat's pajamas has been added to soap. In fact, if I see a "Cat's Pajamas Soap" next time I go to the Farmers Market, I won't be surprised.

Additives are used to change the scent, color, or texture of soap, or to enhance it in some other way—for example, to make it more moisturizing. You don't really need any additives, and for some people, avoiding them is their main reason for making soap in the first place. But others enjoy them, so let's look at some common ones, and you can decide for yourself.

Probably the most common soap additive is scent. The two kinds used most often are *essential oil* and *fragrance oil*.

An e*ssential oil* is an aromatic oil produced from a plant, sometimes diluted with a carrier oil. The plant oil may be distilled with water or steam, or may be extracted with solvents or carbon dioxide.

Some soapmakers prefer essential oils because they're "natural." However, some people are allergic to particular ones. Some are not recommended for use during pregnancy. Some don't work well in soap—for example, the scent of citrus essential oils tends to fade quickly.

If you want to use natural scent but aren't familiar with properties of individual essential oils, I suggest you start with lavender, since it's pleasant, available, and generally safe. Beyond that, research the properties of any essential oil that appeals to you.

Essential oils are available from grocery stores, health food stores, food co-ops, New Age stores, soapmaking supply stores, and Internet sources. Almost all of these except Internet sources sell small quantities at high prices. This is fine for your first batch or two, but after that, save money by checking the Internet. Search on the keywords "essential oils soapmaking" for a long list of suppliers.

A *fragrance oil* is an artificial chemical aroma in a carrier oil. Fragrance oils are supposed to be nontoxic, but like essential oils, they may sometimes cause allergic reactions. *Un*like some essential oils, they don't fade quickly. Some smell great and some are horrible.

Many Internet sources sell fragrance oils. The keywords for a search are "fragrance oils soapmaking." But before you buy any fragrance oil, make sure it's suitable for cold process soap. The seller should state that prominently. Fragrance oils sold at craft stores are for candles and melt-and-pour soap, not for cold-process.

When you open a bottle of essential oil or fragrance oil, especially for the first time, keep the opening turned away from you and/or wear goggles. Once in a long while, the oil from one of these bottles sprays all over.

Colorant for soap is available as either liquid or powder. Of course, a soap mixture will have its own color, created by the colors of the fats and the essential or fragrance oils. So, any color you add will blend with the color already there.

The soap colorant can be either a *pigment* (natural) or a *dye* (artificial). Considerations here are similar to those concerning essential oils versus fragrance oils. Both types of colorant are available from soapmaking suppliers.

You might come across recipes that suggest using crayons or food coloring. Both are nontoxic—but personally, I prefer to use a cosmetic-grade colorant, if I color my soap at all.

Other additives may be used to make the soap harder, make it more moisturizing, increase abrasiveness—you name it. Possibilities include food products such as oatmeal and poppy seed, minerals such as mica and pumice, and decorative or therapeutic flowers and herbs. Some additives—particularly whole plant materials like lavender buds—don't come out of a lye bath as pretty as they went in, so find out how a particular additive works in cold process soap before you try it.

What Do I Use to Make It?
Gathering the Equipment You Need

Though the equipment for soapmaking isn't enormously expensive, there are items you'll definitely need. I've had my share of "Help!" emails from people trying to make do with equipment that just wasn't going to work. They're afraid they won't like soapmaking, so they don't spend money—but it's a self-fulfilling prophecy. A little like trying out ice skating with rollerblades you already have.

Remember my story about my chemistry teacher friend? She said, "Measure correctly, control the temperature, and mix your ingredients well." So, it's no surprise that essential equipment includes a scale for measuring correctly, a thermometer for checking the temperature, and a stick blender for proper mixing. You may already have these tools in your kitchen.

The scale should be digital and should measure in tenths of an ounce, or in grams, or both. You can pay a fortune for a kitchen scale like this in a gourmet shop, but a good postal scale will work just as well and shouldn't be expensive. Such scales are available from office supply stores or on the Web.

Your scale should have a button or control to adjust for *tare*—the weight of the container. Before putting ingredients into a container, place it empty on the scale and push the tare button. The scale will reset to zero. (You may have to push the tare button more than once to make that happen.) Now, when you put in your ingredients, you'll get their weight without the container's.

Another way to eliminate the container weight is to turn the scale off, set the empty container on it, and turn it back on. Again, the display should read zero, and when you add your ingredients, you'll get their weight alone.

Most digital scales use batteries, but some have an optional AC adapter for plugging into an electrical outlet. The adapter is worth the extra cost, since low battery power may cause poor readings and failed soap batches.

To check temperature, you'll need one or two food thermometers—typically the long-stem type used for meat or candy. If you're testing for temperature rise during saponification—as I highly recommend at least for beginners—one thermometer should be digital, "instant-read," and waterproof. Otherwise, digital, dial, or mercury are all fine.

Your optimum temperature range for soapmaking is 90°–110°F (32°–43°C). Any thermometer you use, then, should cover that range and at least ten or twenty degrees Fahrenheit (at least five or ten degrees Celsius) to either side.

A stick blender is a hand-held kitchen gadget, a wand with a blender blade on the end. Other names for it are "immersion blender" and "hand blender." In soapmaking, a stick blender will shorten mixing times from hours to minutes. The recipes and methods in this book assume you're using one.

You can find stick blenders at almost any store that sells small appliances, and often in thrift stores (charity shops, in the U.K.). Currently, my favorite brand is KitchenAid. A more powerful model can shorten your blending times considerably, especially for more difficult recipes like Castile soap.

If you haven't used a stick blender before, take time to learn how it works before you make soap with it. As a safety feature, the power switch must be held in the "on" position for the blender to run. Whenever you let up on the switch, the blade stops.

Try it out first with water. Lower the blade into the liquid before turning on the blender, then let up on the switch before lifting the blade back out. The blade must not be turning as it enters or leaves the liquid, or else the liquid might splatter. Practice until you can handle the switch correctly without thinking.

As I said before, you need gloves and goggles. Lye manufacturers recommend neoprene or PVC gloves. When I started making soap, I bought a pair of chemical gloves from a cleaning-supply store. They're big, thick, and stiff. They work, and they'll probably last longer than I will. But they make it hard to handle things, and being clumsy while working with lye struck me as a problem.

Many soapmakers recommend the more common rubber gloves sold for cleaning and dishwashing. These may be less resistant to lye than chemical gloves would be, but they're more pliable. Personally, I like the extra-long gloves you buy in paint stores to wear while stripping furniture.

Whatever gloves you use, be aware they'll almost surely cut down on your dexterity, so proceed carefully and watch your hands. If the gloves make it hard to press buttons on your scale or microwave, use your knuckle instead of your fingertip.

Goggles are essential. You need the snug-fitting kind worn by woodworkers. Glasses or sunglasses, even the wraparound kind, aren't good enough. Don't take the slightest risk with your eyes. Any hardware store should sell the kind you need, and they're not expensive.

The instructions in this book call for a microwave oven to melt solid fat. Though that's best, you could melt it instead in a slow cooker or in a regular oven at the lowest possible heat.

You also need the following kitchenware:

• Soup pot, stainless steel or enameled steel spatterware, or other large pot. Don't use aluminum—it reacts chemically with lye and may be unsafe. My pot holds about eight quarts (about eight liters), which leaves a good distance between the surface of the soap and the top of the pot. Since the soap mixture must be deep enough to keep the blade of the stick blender submerged, the pot should have a diameter of no more than about eight inches (twenty centimeters) for recipes of the size in this book.

• Saucepan, stainless steel. One that holds two quarts (two liters) is ideal. You could use enameled steel, but it won't work quite as well, as I'll explain later.

• Roasting pan. It doesn't have to be a specific size, but your saucepan should fit into it with room on all sides. Steel is good—ordinary steel, stainless, or enameled. So is heat-resistant plastic. The pan is just to be filled with water and ice, so if you don't have a roasting pan, you can improvise—for example, a lasagna pan will work. Just don't use anything fragile or made of aluminum.

• Large microwave-safe bowl or glass measuring pitcher (large jug, in the U.K.). I prefer a pitcher because I like having the handle and pour spout. Mine holds 10 cups (about two liters). Plastic is fine if it's microwave-safe.

• Bowls or glass measuring cups for weighing lye and fats. I use cups because of the handle and spout. Quart-size (or liter-size) is perfect.

• Two long-handled spoons for stirring—steel, stainless steel, or plastic. For the one used to stir the lye solution, the best choice is a slotted spoon.

• Miscellaneous equipment such as a plastic dishpan, a rubber spatula, and paper towels.

One of the best places to buy much of this kitchenware at a reasonable price is a restaurant supply store. Thrift stores (charity shops) often have good stainless steel and enameled steel cookware. Whatever I need, I check the thrift store first.

When buying used cookware, make sure it isn't aluminum. The name of the material may be stamped on the bottom of the pot. For enameled steel cookware, make sure the interior surfaces are not chipped, or else the exposed metal will stain the soap.

Once your soap mixture is ready, you'll need a mold to pour it into. I'll discuss molds later in detail, but for your first batch, I suggest a milk carton. The best kind is a quart-size (or liter-size) waxed cardboard carton. A half-gallon (two-liter) carton will also do, though the shape of the finished soap will be less than ideal. Plastic milk cartons work fine too. Don't use the silvery-lined paper containers—that lining is aluminum, which reacts chemically with lye.

A milk carton makes a good beginning mold, for reasons of bulk and heat retention. Even if you have small molds for melt-and-pour soap, don't use them for your first batch of cold process.

One more thing you'll need is a way to test your finished soap, to make sure it has no excess lye. The traditional method of testing is to touch the soap for a second with your tongue. This is the soapmaker's version of Russian roulette, and I do *not* recommend it. Even if it wasn't dangerous, there's a reason why washing someone's mouth out with soap is a punishment.

The better way to test is with pH strips or a digital pH meter, both of which measure degrees of acidity or alkalinity. Since a meter is expensive, I use the strips. These are designed to change color according to what they're testing. Match the color to one on the chart that comes with the strips, and you have your measurement.

The most important thing to know about pH strips is that there are several kinds, designed to test different ranges. The strips you need for soap will test in a pH range at least from 7 (neutral) to 11 (too alkaline to use). You can buy such strips from an Internet soapmaking supplier or from a company that sells professional or school lab supplies. Strips sold in swimming pool supply stores won't test in this range, and neither will strips used for aquariums, gardening, or saliva tests.

Different brands of pH strips have slightly different color ranges. Some should be used only under natural light, since an ordinary light bulb may shift the subtle shades of green or tan.

Now let's make soap!

Anne's Shea Butter Supreme

Here is the recipe I recommend for your first efforts at soap-making. It's not only good as a starter, it's also my favorite recipe of all, producing a superb soap.

If you're allergic to nuts or have some other reason to avoid shea butter, start instead with the recipe given later for "All-Veggie Grocery Store Soap #1." That one, though, isn't quite as easy to make, and the finished soap isn't quite as fine.

It's handy to copy this recipe so you don't have to flip pages back and forth as you work through the instructions.

> 10.5 oz (298 g) coconut oil
> 10.5 oz (298 g) olive oil
> 9 oz (255 g) shea butter
> 8 oz (227 g) distilled water
> 4.2 oz (119 g) lye
>
> Scent (optional)—Start with the manufacturer's directions for amount, or use about 1.2 oz (about 35 g). Since aroma strengths and personal tastes vary, figuring how much to use may take trial and error.
>
> Colorant (optional)—Follow the manufacturer's directions for amount.

Before proceeding, read the following pages thoroughly to understand the method!

Step-by-Step Soapmaking
From Prep to Cleanup and Beyond

I've told you that making soap is simple, and it is. There are three basic steps.

1. Prepare the fats.
2. Make a lye solution.
3. Mix the lye solution and the fats.

That's it. Everything else is either preparation, cleanup, or a detail.

Of course, some of the details are important. Not difficult, just important. Many are tricks and shortcuts I've worked out for myself or learned from others who like to simplify soapmaking. These are what make students comment at the end of my class, "I thought it would be more complicated than *that*."

Other details are given just so you won't be left wondering about anything. Don't let them fool you into deciding soapmaking is hard. If you were describing how to make pancakes, you could write pages of details. That doesn't mean it's hard to make pancakes.

The first time you make soap, allow plenty of time— preferably two to three uninterrupted hours. The time you need will decrease dramatically with experience. It takes me about half an hour to make a batch. But you'll be much slower when you're learning, and it's important not to feel rushed.

Now let's look at the whole procedure, from preparation, to cleanup, and beyond.

The Main Work Area

Dressing for Soapmaking

Cover yourself completely for protection—long sleeves, long pants, socks, and solid shoes—using clothes you don't care about. Or wear a protective outer layer, like a lab coat. If you have long hair, tie it back.

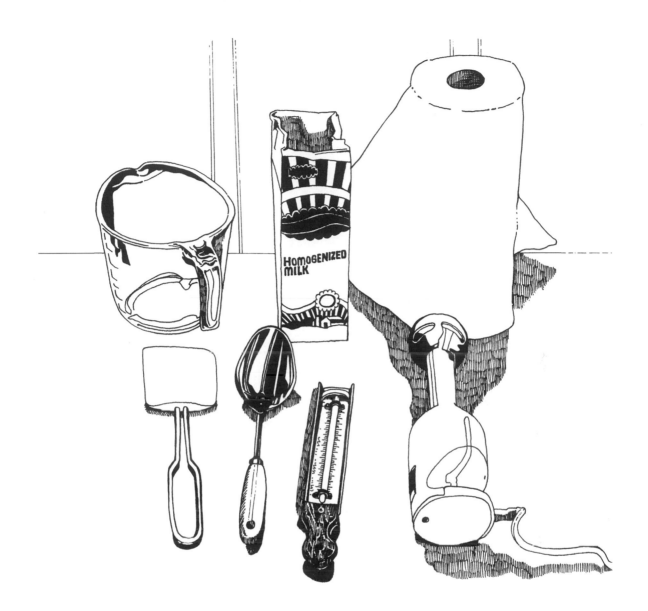

Preparing the Work Areas

For your main work area, the most important requirement is a handy source of running water. I set up in my kitchen, where I can use the sink.

You'll need a special work area for mixing the lye solution. The most important need in this area is good ventilation to remove fumes. Some soapmakers mix the lye outdoors, others work on a stovetop with the range hood fan running at top speed. Wherever your lye mixing area is, keep other people and pets away from it. If you work on a table that's painted or varnished, protect the surface with a tarp or other waterproof covering.

Here's what goes in the main work area:

- Scale.
- Saucepan.
- Soup pot or other large pot.
- Large microwave-safe bowl or glass measuring pitcher for solid fat.
- Bowl or glass measuring cup for lye.
- Bowl or glass measuring cup for each liquid fat. (But skip this item if there's only one kind of liquid fat in the recipe.)
- Small bowls for scent and colorant (if you're using them).
- Food thermometer, preferably waterproof digital "instant-read."
- Stick blender. Plug this in near the sink—to the right of it, if you're right-handed, to the left if you're a lefty. Take the same care you would with any electrical appliance near water. Use a grounded outlet, or if available, a GFI outlet—the kind with a circuit breaker and a reset button built in.
- Long-handled spoon, steel, stainless steel, or plastic.
- Spatula, rubber or silicone.
- Soap mold. As I said before, I recommend a milk carton for your first efforts. If it's cardboard, open the top completely to make a square opening. If it's plastic, cut off the top just below the screw threads, but leave the handle.
- Roll of paper towels.

The Lye Mixing Area

• Vinegar. (This is for cleanup, *not* for lye burns.)

• Plastic dishpan with water for soiled utensils. I pour in some vinegar too. I don't count on the vinegar to neutralize lye, but the smell at least reminds me there's nasty stuff in the dishpan.

• All recipe ingredients (including lye).

Here's what goes in the lye mixing area:

- Roasting pan, stainless or enameled steel.
- Food thermometer. (If you have only one thermometer to share between here and the main work area, place it here first. If you have two, this one has less need to be digital.)
- Long-handled spoon, steel, stainless steel, or plastic—preferably slotted.
- Pitcher of cold or chilled tap water.
- Bowl of ice cubes.
- Roll of paper towels (if you're not by your main work area).

Preparing the Ingredients

1. In your main work area, turn on the scale. Make sure it's set to your choice of ounces or grams.

2. Place the empty saucepan on the scale and push the "tare" button to reset the scale to zero.

3. Pour distilled water into the saucepan till you have the correct weight for your recipe. If you pour too much, don't take the pan off the scale—remove excess water with a spoon.

4. With the same weighing method you just used for the water, weigh the liquid fat from your recipe into the soup pot. Or if you have more than one liquid fat, weigh each one into a separate bowl or cup, then combine the fats in the pot. Using separate containers lets you remove some of an individual fat if you pour too much while measuring.

5. If you're using liquid colorant, add a few drops now.

6. Place the soup pot in the sink.

7. Weigh all solid fat for your recipe into the large microwave-safe bowl or glass measuring pitcher. It's easy to tell solid fats apart and remove a little of one if you add too much, so you

don't need separate containers for two or more fats. Just tare the scale before adding each one—*don't try* to add the weights in your head.

8. Heat the solid fat in your microwave till it's just melted. The time needed depends on the quantity and type of solid fat and also on your microwave. In mine, it takes about two and a half minutes for the solid fat in my starter recipe. Be careful not to overheat. The fat should not boil or smoke. You can leave the melted fat in the microwave for now.

9. If you're using scent, weigh it into a small bowl, using the same technique as for the water and the liquid fat. If your scent came with recommendations for quantity, figure the amount needed for your *batch weight*—meaning the combined weight of all the recipe's fat, without the other ingredients. For all recipes in this book, the batch weight would be 1.8 lb (0.8 kg). If you were given no recommendations, use about 1.2 oz (about 35 g) of scent for this batch weight.

10. If you're using powdered soap colorant, mix it in a small bowl with about a tablespoon (around 15 milliliters) of liquid fat taken from the large soup pot. For my starter recipe, use a quarter to a half teaspoon (around two milliliters) of powder. Blend this mixture to a smooth paste. Don't put it back in the pot yet.

Mixing the Lye Solution

1. PUT ON YOUR GOGGLES AND GLOVES.

2. In your main work area, make sure your bowl or glass cup for measuring lye is completely dry, as is anything else that might contact the lye.

3. Put the bowl or cup on the scale, and tare it back to zero. (If it's hard to work the scale buttons with gloves on, use your knuckle instead of your fingertip.)

4. Weigh the lye for your recipe into a bowl or cup. Note: In rare cases, static electricity will make the lye grains scatter as they're poured. If you see this happening, spoon out the lye instead of pouring it, or first wipe the bowl or cup with a dryer sheet.

5. Take the bowl or cup of lye and the saucepan of distilled water to your lye mixing area. Set the saucepan into the roasting pan.

6. If your lye mixing area is on the stove in your kitchen, turn on your hood fan to top speed and open windows.

7. Trickle the lye gradually into the water in the saucepan, stirring constantly with the long-handled, slotted spoon. Note: You're adding lye to water. *Never add water to lye.* I've seen more than one set of soapmaking instructions get this wrong! (Since I promised I'd tell you if I passed along information without experimenting, I have to say I haven't tried adding water to lye. It's enough for me that the U.S. Consumer Product Safety Commission recalled a soapmaking book for giving that advice.)

As the lye dissolves, the solution will heat up and give off fumes. If you're working outdoors, stay upwind. If you're in your kitchen, stand away from the solution, keep the vent fan running, and keep the windows open. Some people are unusually sensitive to lye fumes, and no one finds them pleasant. For most people, the fumes from a small batch like the one from my starter recipe won't be a problem. Just don't get too close or let them collect.

Try to keep the lye from forming a crust on the bottom of the saucepan. You want the lye to dissolve as you add it. If a crust does form, grate it with the back of the slotted spoon. Be careful not to splash.

Scrape the last of the lye from your bowl or cup with the spoon, then keep stirring till the lye is thoroughly dissolved. The solution will be cloudy at first, then turn clear. Even after that, a few grains of lye can remain, so keep stirring till they're all gone.

8. Pour your cold or chilled water from the pitcher into the roasting pan—*not* into the saucepan with the lye solution. Make the water in the roasting pan as deep as possible without floating the saucepan, then add ice cubes to the roasting pan. This bath will quickly cool the lye solution, especially if your saucepan is stainless steel instead of enameled. Stirring the solution will help cool it even faster, and so will lifting the saucepan slightly so the ice water contacts the pan's bottom.

9. Check the temperature by holding the thermometer in the lye solution without letting it touch the bottom of the saucepan. You want the solution to be in the range of 90°–110°F (32°–43°C).

10. When the solution has cooled enough, take the saucepan of lye solution and your other lye utensils to your main work area. Don't try to carry too much at once! Put those other lye utensils into the plastic dishpan of vinegar water.

As I said earlier in this book, you're extremely unlikely to burn yourself or anyone else with lye if you just follow directions, pay attention, and use gloves and goggles. But if it does happen, flush the burn with cold running water for at least fifteen minutes, with any contaminated clothing removed. Lye manufacturers recommend that you then call a doctor or poison control center for further help.

Combining the Ingredients

1. Take the fat you melted and pour it into the soup pot with the liquid fat. (If the melted fat has been sitting for very long, it might be good to reheat it a bit.) Combining the fats should bring them almost at once into the desired range of 90°–110°F (32°–43°C).

2. Pour the lye solution into the soup pot with the fat. The lye solution and the fat do NOT have to be at identical temperatures, but the final mixture should be somewhere in the range of 90°–110°F (32°–43°C).

3. Stir briefly but well with the long-handled spoon to start mixing the ingredients.

4. Carefully check the temperature with the thermometer and make a note of it. (Again, it's best if the thermometer is waterproof, "instant-read," and digital.)

5. Mix with the stick blender. Move it through the mixture so everything gets mixed thoroughly, tipping the pan as you need to. While the blender is running, be careful to keep the blade submerged, or you'll stir a lot of air into the soap and may splash the mixture. When you lift the blade out of the mixture, take your finger off the button so the blade stops before reaching the surface.

You'll soon see changes in the mixture. Originally oily and transparent, it will become creamy and opaque. The surface, which was shiny at first, will become duller, and the oily ring at the edge of the mixture's surface—right where it meets the wall of the pot—will shrink and all but disappear.

Next you'll notice the mixture thickening and getting smoother. It will come to resemble thick eggnog or very thin pudding. At this point, you can stop blending, because the saponification that produces soap can continue without further mixing. You might call this the "point of no return." (As I said before, with the stick blender, you *don't* have to keep mixing long enough to see "trace," as other instructions might call for.)

Besides these visual signs, you can get a feel for the thickness by turning off the blender and briefly stirring with it like a spoon. With a weaker blender, you can even *hear* the difference, as the thickening slows down the blade, causing the sound of the motor to drop in pitch.

The final sign for you is temperature. When you notice the mixture growing thicker and smoother, start checking it again with your thermometer. Saponification generates heat, and by the time the mixture has reached the "point of no return," the temperature should have risen about a couple of degrees Fahrenheit (one degree Celsius). Once it has, you're done!

An experienced soapmaker can do without this temperature test, but I highly recommend it at least for your first few tries while you learn the other signs—especially if you're not working with a teacher. Beyond that, though, it's always a great final check.

How long should you be blending? That depends a good deal on the power of your motor. With a powerful blender, the appearance can start changing almost at once, and you can notice thickening within a few minutes. With a weaker blender, you might see little difference at all for five or ten minutes, or even longer with a difficult recipe.

You should have little trouble recognizing the signs I've given—but if you're not sure, it doesn't hurt to blend some more. You'll want to stop, though, by the time the temperature has risen five degrees Fahrenheit (three degrees Celsius). Just a few degrees above that, the mixture can suddenly become too thick to pour from the pot!

6. Add any scent or colorant you've made ready, and blend a bit to mix it in.

7. Pour the mixture into your mold, scraping the pot with the rubber spatula. If your mold is a cardboard milk carton, close the flaps exactly as they were when unopened and fasten them shut. If the carton is too full to close, or if you're using a plastic milk container, cover the top loosely with plastic wrap. Label the carton or container. You don't want anyone to mistake this for milk.

8. Put your mold aside to sit awhile—somewhere out of the cat's or the kids' reach. The soap will continue to saponify while it's sitting. This reaction will keep generating heat as it goes on—so if you happen to notice the soap and mold getting warmer, don't worry about it. They're supposed to!

Cleanup

1. Don't take off your gloves and goggles till you're finished cleaning up.

2. If you use a dishwasher, wash your utensils once by hand before loading them. If you don't, your dishwasher will probably run over. If you're washing *only* by hand, wash twice. Pay special attention to handles and the outer lip of the pot.

3. Wipe down your work surfaces with a paper towel dampened with the vinegar.

4. Wash your gloves *with your hands still inside them.*

5. *Now* take off your gloves and goggles.

Removal and Testing

Your soap should be solid in about twelve hours, and ready to come out of the mold and be tested in about twenty-four. You'll know that the saponification is mostly complete because the soap and mold will have cooled to room temperature. If your mold is a milk carton, you can also squeeze it to make sure the soap is solid. If it is, put on your gloves, then tear or cut away the carton.

At this point, the soap shouldn't be caustic, but you should keep your gloves on till you test it. Put a little distilled water on its surface, scrub it around to make a paste, then push a pH strip into the paste. If the strip shows anything in the range of 7 to 10, the soap is fine. The exact pH reading doesn't matter—the strips don't measure all that accurately anyway. But they *will* let you know if your soap is in a safe range.

If the pH strip reads 11 or 12, let the soap sit for a few days and test it again. It may just need a little more time. If your reading is above 12, don't use the soap and don't even touch it without gloves. Sometimes a very high pH will slowly decrease till the soap is usable. More often, the soap should be discarded or rebatched. (See my chapter on frequently asked questions for info on rebatching.)

If your soap is in a block—as it will be if you used a milk carton—then start your testing on the outside surface. If that tests OK, slice the block in half with a large, sharp knife such as a French cook's knife.

Look at the cut surfaces. Your soap should have a texture that's fairly smooth and regular, with a consistency like cheese. It may be slightly sticky on the cut edges, and there may be a small difference in texture between the cut faces and the outer surface of the block—something like a rind covering a soft cheese. This is normal.

Finish by testing one of the cut surfaces with a pH strip. If it tests OK, you're home free.

It's important to test for safety's sake, but don't let me scare you. If you follow the instructions in this book and use recipes that are properly designed, you should *never* see a pH reading that's dangerously high.

Cutting and Curing

After testing, remove your gloves, take your large, sharp knife, and finish slicing the soap into bars. If you like, you can trim the sides to make them neater. You can also smooth the edges by beveling them with a vegetable peeler.

Soap should dry out for a while, which also gives it a chance to grow milder. Set the bars in a well-ventilated area, on a rack if possible. Drying time depends on how much water the soap was made with, as well as on how it's stored and the humidity of the storage area. Minimum times normally range from a couple of weeks to a month, with most of the recipes in this book falling about halfway between. Soap with a very high percentage of liquid fat may need to dry even longer.

How can you be sure the soap is dry enough? Just try a bar. If it gets used up too fast or gets gooey, that soap needs more time. The longer the bars dry—up to a couple of months or so—the harder they'll be and the longer they'll last in use.

More Recipes!
Different Soaps You Can Try

Many books give you numerous recipes that are really only a couple of soaps dressed up with different scents and colors. Instead, I'll now give you a variety of basic soaps that are easy to make. Creative choices of scent and appearance remain for you—a visit to the Web site of any major soapmaking supplier will probably give you enough inspiration to last about five years.

My recipes include a good assortment of soaps that use only grocery or health food store fats. Other recipes call for fats that probably are available only from soapmaking suppliers. Good sources are listed in the resources section of this book, and you may be lucky enough to find a local vendor. Local prices are often higher, but count shipping costs when you compare.

If you're making soap for others, be aware that some people are highly allergic to particular fats.

All my recipes use 30 oz of fat (850 g). You need a soap mold that will hold at least 5 cups (1.2 l) of liquid.

Follow the directions I've already given, unless a recipe calls for a variation.

Recipe Checking

Before you try a new soap recipe—mine or anyone else's—always check the given lye and water amounts to make sure they're correct. Even if the recipe comes from a published book, don't use it till you're sure it has no errors—and that goes double for any recipe you find on the Internet.

Though you can do the math yourself, the simplest and safest way to check a recipe is with a *lye calculator*. These tell you how much lye and water you should use for a given quantity of fat. Many such calculators can be found and used on the Web for free, and they're found in some computer programs as well. I've listed some of both kinds in the resources section, along with Web sites that explain how to calculate by hand.

All-Veggie Grocery Store Soap #1

This is an excellent basic soap with easily available ingredients.

      9 oz (255 grams) coconut oil
      21 oz (595 grams) olive oil
      9 oz (255 grams) distilled water
      4.1 oz (116 grams) lye

All-Veggie Grocery Store Soap #2

This soap is a little softer than average, but you might not even notice the difference. It has good lather and is moisturizing. Careful with this one—allergy to peanuts is common. (Outside North America, corn oil—sometimes known as "maize oil"—may not be as readily available.)

   3.5 oz (99 g) peanut oil
   17.5 oz (496 g) corn oil
   7 oz (198 g) coconut oil
   7 oz (198 g) distilled water
   3.8 oz (108 g) lye

Grocery Store Shortening Soap

This soap has good hardness and lather but is below average in moisturizing. I'd use it where moisturizing is less important than cleaning power.

This recipe calls for Crisco, a popular American brand of vegetable shortening. In other parts of the world, you can safely substitute any other shortening made of soy and cottonseed oils. (The proportions don't matter too much, because lye requirements of the two oils are nearly identical.)

20 oz (567 g) Crisco
10 oz (284 g) coconut oil
10 oz (284 g) distilled water
4.3 oz (122 g) lye

Non-Veggie Grocery Store Soap

A harder-than-average soap with average lather. Average in moisturizing.

      8.4 oz (238 g) lard
      9.8 oz (278 g) coconut oil
      9.8 oz (278 g) olive oil
      8 oz (227 g) distilled water
      4 oz (113 g) lye

Olive Palm Soap

A slightly harder soap with good lather and moisturizing.

      18 oz (510 g) olive oil
      12 oz (340 g) palm kernel oil
      9 oz (255 g) distilled water
      4.1 oz (116 g) lye

Chris's Avocado Soap

A moisturizing soap with average lather. I designed this for my friend Chris, who asked for soap with avocado oil.

- 2.5 oz (71 g) avocado butter
- 7.5 oz (213 g) coconut oil
- 12.5 oz (354 g) avocado oil
- 7.5 oz (213 g) olive oil
- 9 oz (255 g) distilled water
- 4.1 oz (116 g) lye

Aaron's Hazelnut Soap

This soap lathers very well and is highly moisturizing. Do not insulate or warm this soap as it's setting. I designed it for my husband, Aaron, and scented it with hazelnut fragrance, which he loves.

17.5 oz (496 g) hazelnut oil
10.5 oz (298 g) palm kernel oil
8 oz (227 g) distilled water
3.9 oz (111 g) lye

Almond Facial Soap

This soap lathers beautifully and is highly moisturizing. Since this recipe contains only liquid fats, the method is slightly different. Put the fats into the microwave-safe pitcher and warm them to just 100°F (38°C). They'll reach that temperature quickly—in less than a minute in my microwave. Don't try to use regular coconut oil here—it must be fractionated!

5.9 oz (167 g) fractionated coconut oil
22.1 oz (627 g) almond oil
7 oz (198 g) distilled water
4.1 oz (116 g) lye

Variation: Increase the water to 8 oz (227 g) and pour into a mug for use as shaving soap.

Anne's Longer-Lasting Soap

This is a fairly hard soap that works well where softer soaps get sticky. Since all the fats in this recipe are solid, you'll need to modify the basic method a little. One way is to heat all the fats together till they're melted, then cool to about 110°F (43°C). Or you can melt all the fats except the coconut oil and then combine them. Either way, you're working at the high end of the usual temperature range, which prevents the fat from solidifying on its own during processing.

    1.5 oz (43 g) cocoa butter
    6 oz (170 g) avocado butter
    10.5 oz (298 g) palm oil
    6 oz (170 g) coconut oil
    6 oz (170 g) shea butter
    9 oz (255 g) distilled water
    4 oz (113 g) lye

Designing Your Own
How to Create Great Recipes

Once you've made good soap from one or two of my recipes, you may be eager to design your own. It really isn't hard if you spend a little time learning about various fats and additives. You'll also want to become familiar with lye calculators and other soapmaking design tools.

Write down everything you try. This will help you learn what works and what doesn't, and to repeat what works especially well.

Start small. Though smaller quantities force you to be especially careful with measurements, you avoid having a huge batch of something that didn't work.

Choosing Fats

Choosing a blend of fats for a new recipe requires some thought. Each fat is chemically unique, which is why soap made from one fat or blend may be quite different from another. The qualities that most concern soapmakers are fluffy lather, stable lather, soap hardness, and moisturizing.

Some fats produce soap with fluffy lather—the soapmaker's term for large, abundantly-produced bubbles similar to those from commercial bars. Although fluffy lather has little to do with how well the soap cleans, it's a pleasant quality that you'll probably favor. The disadvantage of such fats is that most of them tend to dry the skin. Some of the best fats for fluffy lather are coconut oil and palm kernel oil.

Some fats produce soap with stable lather, which is denser and creamier. As a rule, these fats are more moisturizing than the ones that make soap with fluffy lather. However, some people dislike this kind of lather—a factor if you're making soaps for others. Good fats for stable lather are olive oil, sweet almond oil, and corn oil (sometimes called maize oil).

Some fats make soap that's harder and lasts longer. Among the best fats for hardness are tallow (beef fat), coconut oil, and palm kernel oil.

Some fats make soap that dries the skin, others are more moisturizing, or *emollient*. Some of the best fats for moisturizing are apricot kernel oil, sweet almond oil, shea butter, and olive oil.

Your choices may depend on practical considerations. Some fats are expensive, others quite cheap. Some are available in every grocery store, others are harder to find. Some fats are just more difficult to make into soap.

A rule of thumb is that at least 40% of a soap's fat should be solid. Like all rules of thumb, this one has exceptions. One of the oldest soap formulas, Castile soap, traditionally was made from one hundred percent olive oil. It is, however, notoriously hard to make. And a recipe with all its fat polyunsaturated won't make soap easily, and may not make good soap at all.

Each of the soapmaking fats has its strengths and weaknesses. If you want to design your own recipes, learn the properties of different fats and try different combinations.

Superfatting, Lye Discount, Water Range

I've already recommended using a lye calculator to check all new recipes before you try them. Of course, you'll use one too when designing your own recipe, to tell you how much lye and water you'll need.

A term you're likely to run into when using one of these calculators is *lye discount*. Let's take a look at what this means.

In the chemical reaction that makes soap, the lye is neutralized by the fat. If you used only exactly enough fat for this neutralizing, there would be no margin for error or for inconsistency in your ingredients. It would be easy for your soap to turn out with too much lye. So we use a little extra fat as a buffer. This is called *superfatting,* and recipes usually have it built in. About 5% to 8% superfatting is the norm.

Lye discount is another way to refer to this. Most lye calculators figure in this discount as a default. But be careful to check this. A few will give a zero lye discount, which will put your soap—at best—right on the edge of being lye heavy.

Most lye calculators also give water quantity as a range. With the least water, you get faster saponification and faster curing. But then it's a little harder to dissolve the lye, and the solution may give off more fumes.

For a reasonable drying time, you definitely want to use the least water if less than 40% of the fat in your recipe is solid. On the other hand, if your scent is one that speeds up saponification—"accelerates trace," as the suppliers say—you may get better results with the most water.

The Mysteries of INS

In the early 1900s, chemists figured out a way to roughly predict the hardness of soap when made from a given fat or blend. The indicator they came up with is called the *INS value*.

Those initials stand for "Iodine Number Saponification Value." The *iodine number* is a measure of how unsaturated a fat is, while the *saponification value* is used to figure how much lye is needed to convert that fat to soap. The INS value is the saponification value minus the iodine number. Values range from less than zero to over 250. The higher the number, the greater the hardness the soap is supposed to have.*

Very few handcraft soapmakers are chemists, so not many had even heard of INS values till Dr. Robert S. McDaniel wrote about them in his excellent 2000 book *Essentially Soap.* Without really explaining what the values stood for, McDaniel did say that any blend of fats with a value near 160 should produce an ideal soap.

For myself, I wouldn't call a soap ideal without also considering the properties of the fats and the soap's intended use. But from my experiments, an INS value in the range of 145 to 160 does predict easy saponification. In other words, if your mixture has a value in that range, you should get it to turn into soap without much fuss. And if its value is not close to that range, the recipe may either be troublesome or make poor soap. Or both.

So, INS values can be a great help in figuring whether your exciting new idea for a soap recipe is likely to work. Later,

---

* The information on the origin and purpose of INS comes from "The History of the Manufacture of Soap," by F. W. Gibbs, in *Annals of Science,* Vol. 4, Issue 2, April 15, 1939. You didn't miss that issue, did you?

when you get a better feel for various fats and the way they work together, you may not need INS—some advanced recipe designers pay no attention to it, even if they did at first—but you can always fall back on it in a pinch.

To get the INS value for a blend of fats, you have to use an INS calculator or do a little arithmetic. A table of INS values follows this chapter. To calculate by hand, look up the value of each fat from the recipe and make a chart like this:

Fat	Weight (oz)	INS
Palm kernel oil	12	235
Olive oil	18	109

Add the weights of each fat to get the total weight. In this case, we have:

12 oz + 18 oz = 30 oz

Next, divide the weight of the palm kernel oil by the total weight:

12 oz ÷ 30 oz = 0.4

Multiply this number by the INS value for palm kernel oil and round the answer to the nearest whole number:

0.4 x 235 = 94

The same calculation for the olive oil gives you 65.
Now add your answers to get the INS value for the blend:

94 + 65 = 159

You can see this is nearly the ideal INS value of 160. A fat blend with this value should be easy to make into soap. And in fact, this blend produces a very nice soap, which you'll find as one of the recipes in this book.

Just the same, you can't judge a fat or blend just by its INS value. You still need to take into account all properties of individual fats. Using a good soapmaking program or Web-based design tool is the best way to make sure your fats provide good hardness, moisturizing, and lather. See the resources section of this book for several listings.

The values in the following table were mostly calculated from saponification values and iodine numbers I found on various suppliers' Web sites. Note that the INS value for each type of fat can vary from one batch to another—so, if your supplier lists a value, use that instead.

If you can't get the INS value from your supplier or this table, you can often find the other values to calculate INS yourself. As I said before, it's figured by subtracting the iodine number from the saponification value—most often called "SAP value" or "SAP number."

Confusingly, saponification values are found in two different versions. The ones you want are the "big" ones with whole numbers. The other kind, with decimal values less than 1, cannot easily be used to calculate INS.

INS Values Table

Almond oil	97
Aloe butter	238
Apricot kernel oil	91
Avocado oil	103
Avocado butter	130
Babassu oil	234
Beeswax	84
Black cumin seed oil	72
Baobab oil	98
Borage oil	49
Camelina seed oil	44
Canola oil	70
Castor oil	95
Cocoa butter	158
Coconut oil (plain, "76°")	248
Coconut oil, fractionated	324
Corn oil (maize oil)	71
Cottonseed oil	88
Crisco	111
Emu oil	125

Evening primrose oil	38
Grapeseed oil	66
Hazelnut oil	101
Hemp oil	40
Illipe butter	153
Jojoba oil	9
Karanja oil	96
Kokum butter	154
Kukui nut oil	25
Lanolin	83
Lard (pig fat)	125
Linseed oil (flax)	−3
Macadamia nut oil	120
Mango butter	137
Mango oil	138
Meadowfoam oil	88
Mink oil	105
Mowrah butter	130
Neem tree oil	118
Olive oil	109
Palm oil	148
Palm kernel oil	235
Passion fruit seed oil	63

Peach kernel oil	87
Peanut oil	93
Perilla seed oil	0
Pistachio oil	106
Poppy seed oil	57
Rapeseed oil	69
Rice bran oil	82
Rose hip oil	−7
Safflower oil	48
Safflower oil, high linoleic	100
Sal butter	146
Sesame oil	79
Shea butter	112
Shea oil	100
Soybean oil	62
Stearic acid	209
Sunflower oil	58
Sunflower oil, high oleic	102
Tallow (beef fat)	159
Tamanu oil	84
Walnut oil	42
Wheat germ oil	58

Getting Your Soap in Shape
How to Choose or Make a Mold

Soap molds come in an infinite variety of shapes and sizes. So, it's best to put off thinking about them till you've made a soap batch or two. Your ideas of what kind you want will probably be changed by your first efforts.

For the recipes in this book, you'll need a mold that holds 5 cups (1.2 l) of water.

Kinds of Mold

Various household objects can be used for soap molds. Many beginners use cardboard or wood boxes, baking pans, plastic food containers—just about anything you can imagine. For individual bars, the "snack size" disposable/reusable food storage containers make great molds. The ones I buy have a maximum capacity of about a cup and a half (about one-third liter), though you won't fill them completely. They make a large, easy-to-hold bar with an attractive raised border.

Good materials for "found" molds include wood, glass, plastic, silicone, and stainless steel. If you use cardboard, it must be sturdy. Keep in mind that the object's shape must allow the soap to be removed easily. Loaf pans, brownie pans, and wood boxes are objects that work well for that.

Several kinds of soap mold are sold by craft stores and soapmaking suppliers. The most familiar kind is the molded plastic tray with compartments for three or four individual bars. Craft stores sell these for working with melt-and-pour soap, but some soapmakers like them for cold process as well. I don't, because I dislike the extra fuss of pouring individual bars, and I've had trouble getting the soap out.

Tray molds are large, shallow boxes, one bar in depth. They may include ornamental patterns, as well as raised lines that make grooves in the soap to guide cutting it into individual bars. Or they may have removable dividers that separate your mixture into bar-sized portions after you've poured it. Baking pans can be used as tray molds—just don't use aluminum.

Block or *loaf molds,* such as simple wood boxes, make a thick block of soap to be sliced into bars. This is the easiest kind to use, and it's also easy to make. For the recipes in this book, you could build one with a cavity about 4 in. high, 3 in. wide, and 7 in. long (about 10 cm high, 8 cm wide, and 18 cm long).

Lining a Soap Mold

To be sure you can remove the soap, line any mold that can't be taken apart or destroyed. Some books say that soap can be removed easily from flexible molds such as plastic food containers. In my experience, that's sometimes true, but not always.

Molds made of absorbent materials—such as wood or cardboard—all need to be lined. Others may as well if they're inflexible or have complex shapes. As with so much in soapmaking, the need for lining may depend on the recipe. A high percentage of liquid fat makes your soap likely to stick.

Good lining materials include:

- Pieces of plastic tarp
- Freezer paper (with the shiny side toward the soap)

- Plastic bags that fit your mold (with any printing on the side away from the soap)
- Parchment paper
- Plastic wrap

DO NOT USE ALUMINUM FOIL. It reacts with lye.

With plastic linings, the heavier the plastic, the fewer the wrinkles in the surface of your soap. For instance, the trash bags meant as liners for outdoor garbage cans will work better than the smaller, thinner-walled ones that you'd use in your kitchen.

An easy way to make a liner is to use two overlapping rectangles. For instance, I've used pieces of plastic tarp to line box molds—one rectangle laid into the box lengthwise, another crosswise. Each was long enough to cover the bottom and two sides, with enough left at the top to fold over and cover the poured soap.

But don't use a pieced liner in a mold that is made to come apart, even if you tape the liner pieces together. For such a mold, you need a liner that can't leak. A plastic bag works, if you can find one in a good size. For instance, a gallon-size food bag might do it.

A block mold can be lined safely with one large sheet of paper. Here's the easiest way to do this, as also shown in the illustrations.

1. Cut a Styrofoam block so it just fits the length and width of the inside of the soap mold but rises above it by an inch or so (a couple of centimeters or so). In other words, the block should fill the mold exactly like a block of soap except that it sticks out the top.

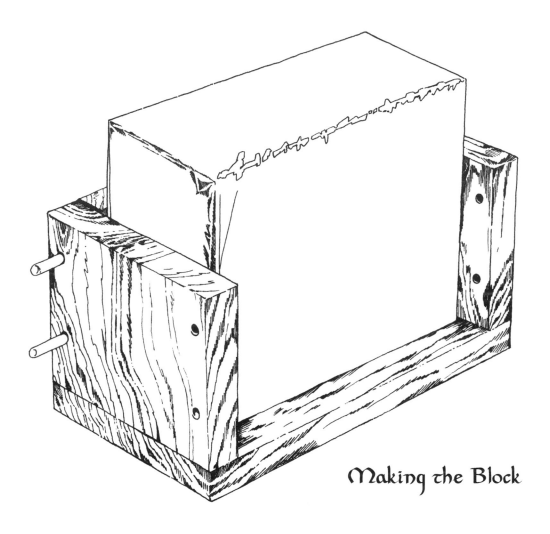

Making the Block

2. Styrofoam is crumbly, and you don't want bits of it in your soap. So, cover the block with plastic wrap and tape it securely.

3. Measure the inside of your mold and use the measurements to cut a sheet from a roll of freezer paper. The width of the paper should be equal to the width of the mold interior plus two times its height, plus about an inch (about a couple of

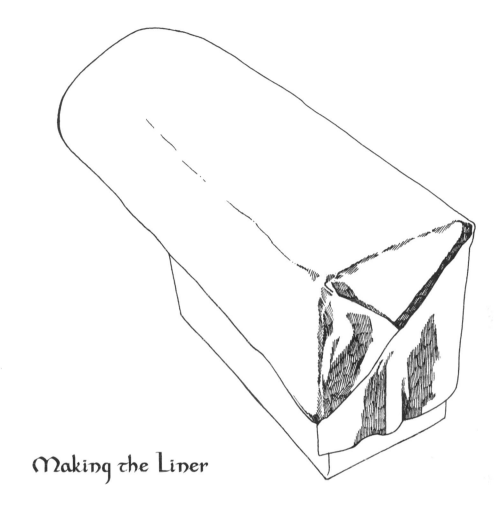

Making the Liner

centimeters) for slack. The length of the paper should be equal to the length of the mold interior plus two times its height, plus about an inch (a couple of centimeters) for slack.

As an example, take a mold with a cavity that's 4 in. high, 3 in. wide, and 7 in. long (the dimensions I recommended earlier).

The width of the paper would be:

Interior width	3 in
Interior height x 2	8 in
Slack	1 in
Total	12 in

The length of the paper would be:

Interior length	7 in
Interior height x 2	8 in
Slack	1 in
Total	16 in

4. Cut out a second, identical sheet of freezer paper, using the first as a pattern. Set one of the sheets aside as a pattern for more liners in the future.

5. Take the other sheet and center it over the block as it stands upright. The shiny side of the paper should be down. Now fold in both sides of the paper, wrapping the block exactly as if you were wrapping a present, except that the bottom surface of the block won't be covered. You can secure the folded ends at first with straight pins stuck through the paper into the Styrofoam. Avoiding pin heads, tape the folded ends of the paper with packing tape, then remove the pins.

6. Remove the paper liner, turn it over, and set it into the soap mold. You can trim the excess from the height if you're using a top on your mold.

7. If necessary, use dabs of shortening to stick the liner to itself at folds, or to the soap mold. This may make the liner fit more neatly and avoid irregularities in the shape of the soap.

8. Keep the Styrofoam block for the next time you make liners.

Complex molds may be lined with plastic wrap. If the pattern in the mold is too fancy to line without losing detail, you can try to use the mold without a lining. Some molds will release the soap if you put them, soap and all, into the freezer for about an hour. Be warned: Sometimes this works and sometimes it doesn't.

Since petroleum jelly and mineral oil will not saponify, some soapmakers use them to grease molds, much as a cook would use shortening to grease a cake pan. Others feel these products leave an undesirable residue on the soap.

Wrapping It Up
Lovely Packaging for Your Soap

You may not be interested in packaging soap for your own use, but as I mentioned before, handcrafted soap makes an ideal gift. And a nice presentation with attractive packaging is a great finishing touch.

You don't want to wrap cold process soap in plastic or food wrap, because that would keep moisture from escaping. What's used instead is a "cigar band." This is a belt-like strip of paper or cloth around the middle of the bar. You can make a cigar band from any attractive paper or fabric.

To add text and/or graphics, use a stick-on label. Address labels are a good size, and they come either in white or transparent. A word processing program will make labels to print from your computer, but a dedicated label making program will probably be easier to use. I mention one in the resources section of this book, but some of the dozens of others are surely as good.

The label might describe the scent and list some of the ingredients. Unless you're sure the person getting the soap has no allergies, you should at least note the fats used in the recipe. (This is assuming you're labeling soap just for gifts. If you're selling it, your label text must comply with labeling laws, and that's a whole subject unto itself.)

For graphics, free clip art is everywhere. The problem is, most of it looks exactly like free clip art. Why not use your own photos instead? You could take pictures of flowers that have the scents you're using, or a seashell to suggest an ocean scent, and so on. A label making program should be able to insert your digital or scanned photo like any other graphic.

Or use a graphics program to create your own designs. Besides several good general programs, some wonderful specialty ones are available. One of my favorites is a program for quilt design. Original quilt designs make lovely labels for soap.

Instead of making a cigar band, you can gift-wrap soap with fabric. Cut your rectangle with pinking shears for a finished appearance. Secure the ends and edges with fabric glue or tacky glue.

Or cut a fabric circle and draw it up around the soap as a bag, tying the opening with a ribbon and letting the top edges form a frill. Tie a label tag to the ribbon. You can make good tags with perforated sheets of business cards meant for computer printing. Scrapbooking and miniatures suppliers sell paper punches that will make only a tiny hole in your label, making it look more professional.

A circular wrapping in nylon net or tulle is also good. The net wrapping is left on when using the soap. This is particularly good for soap that doesn't lather well, since it will increase the lather dramatically.

You can cut net circles yourself or else buy them precut in the bridal section of a craft store. Fasten the top with a transparent rubber band and tie the decorative ribbon over it, as a ribbon alone will come off in use. Transparent rubber bands are sold as hair fasteners, so look for them anywhere you'd buy barrettes. You can also sew the top closed and tie a ribbon over the stitching.

For shaving soap, use a pottery mug as a container and add an old-fashioned shaving brush.

Soap and baskets go together perfectly. Since soap is a consumable gift, it's nice to complement it with something permanent like a basket.

Good packaging will give your soaps the professional look they deserve. It makes all the difference between a gift that looks "homemade" and one that's "handcrafted."

Why, Why, Why?
Frequently Asked Questions

Why do your recipes make such small batches?

Personally, I've never wanted to make much soap of the same scent at once, even when I was making soap as a business. But there are practical advantages too. Smaller batches are easier to mix when you use a stick blender. They produce less lye fumes, so you can work indoors with no problem. The containers are easier to heft around, so there's less chance of an accident. And since smaller quantities of ingredients are at risk, a beginner will be less afraid of failure.

All in all, I think it's best for a beginner to start small. But smaller batches do have one disadvantage: Precise measurement is more critical.

If you want to make larger batches, increase the amount of each fat proportionally, then use a lye calculator to re-figure the amounts of lye and water. The water and lye you need to add are *not* proportional to the added fat.

With *much* larger batches, you might also have to watch out for overheating in the mold. Using a stick blender means there's more heat generated after the mixture has been poured than there would be with hand stirring. If there's too much bulk and the heat can't leave the mold fast enough, the soap mixture could even reach the boiling point. So, if your batch is very large, you should still stick with molds of moderate size—and if you're filling a number of them at once, make sure to leave space between them.

Your recipes measure ounces down to a tenth. Why aren't you that exact with grams?

Since there are about 28 grams to an ounce, measuring in whole grams is actually more precise than measuring in tenths of an ounce.

Why do you use coconut oil in so many recipes?

It's true that coconut oil is expensive in grocery-store quantities and that many stores don't even stock it. But it's still the only grocery store fat that produces good fluffy lather.

What is fractionated oil? If I don't have that kind, can I just use the regular oil?

No, the properties are different. To start with, fractionated oil has a lower melting point, remaining liquid at lower temperatures. In fact, that's what fractionation is all about.

Each natural fat is really made up of many kinds of fat mixed together. To fractionate it, it's first melted (if it isn't already liquid), and then cooled. At some point in the cooling, parts with a higher melting point become solid and drop to the bottom, while parts with a lower melting point are still liquid. The liquid that's skimmed off is the *fractionated oil.*

Sometimes oil is fractionated without being called that. For instance, shea oil is created by fractionating shea butter.

How do I substitute other ingredients for the ones in your recipes?

Whoa. You don't substitute in a soap recipe, you develop a new one. Learn by making your first few batches with tried-and-true recipes. You can get as creative as you want—later.

Why do you recommend distilled water for soapmaking and pH testing?

Minerals in tap, well, or spring water can affect both soapmaking and testing. Some such water would probably work, but you can't predict it. Even long-ago country soapmakers—who were mostly completely unscientific—often relied on rainwater, nature's closest equivalent to distilled.

Why weigh the water? I can just use a measuring cup.

It's true that, for water, fluid ounces for measuring volume and ounces for measuring weight are more or less equivalent (more in the U.K., less in the U.S.). And since using a precise amount of water isn't critical in soapmaking, measuring by sight in a cup will work. But weighing is more accurate, and less trouble too, I think. In any case, the equivalence of the ounces is *for water only*. Don't try this for anything else.

Why do you use a stainless steel saucepan for mixing the lye solution? Everyone else says to use a glass measuring cup. Also, what's the roasting pan of tap water for?

When you add lye to water, the solution gets hot. It can get up to boiling. For cold process soapmaking such as I describe, it should be in the range of 90°–110°F (32°–43°C). In a glass container, getting back down to that range takes it forever. With the stainless steel container and a cold water bath, reaching that range takes it only a minute or two, even in hot weather.

Why is it so important to add the lye to the water instead of the other way around? I've seen sources that say you can add water to lye.

One or two books and a few Web sites say to add water to lye. DON'T DO IT. Adding water to lye is dangerous, because the reaction is so strong. The U.S. Consumer Product Safety Commission actually recalled one soapmaking book for giving this advice.* We're also warned not to add lye to warm or hot water, again because of the strong reaction.

I read that I should keep a bottle of vinegar handy in case I get lye on myself. Why don't you recommend that?

Treating the burn with vinegar will make it worse. The vinegar will neutralize the lye but will generate heat and further damage your skin. Lye manufacturers recommend that you use running water.

Your instructions are for a microwave oven, but what if I don't have one?

You can melt the solid fat in a slow cooker, or in a regular oven at the lowest possible heat. Either of these will take forty-five minutes to an hour to melt the solid fats in my starter recipe (including the coconut oil). Get them melted completely before proceeding.

I don't recommend melting fat on a stovetop. Not that you *can't* do it, and do it safely. But there are a lot of "if's"—*if* you use a double boiler, *if* you pay close and constant attention, *if* you're prepared to handle a grease fire if one starts. I don't do it, and again, I don't recommend it.

Why can't I use a plastic pail for mixing the lye solution with the fat? What about other plastic utensils?

I can't exactly recommend "plastic," because plastics are all different. Some soapmakers say that plastic works fine. But you do have to be sure it's heat-resistant. If the container is

---

* See U.S. Consumer Product Safety Commission Release #04-010, October 15, 2003. Find the notice on the commission's Web site at www.cpsc.gov.

microwave-safe, it should be OK. Or fill it with boiling water to see if it gets soft.

Why use a stick blender? Why not just stir with a spoon? Or what about an electric mixer or a regular blender?

The stick blender is ideal for mixing the fat with the lye solution quickly, thoroughly, and safely. You *can* use a spoon. If you do, be prepared to stir for a *long* time.

Special soapmaking recipes and techniques for electric mixers and regular blenders can be found on the Web. I'm not an expert in making soap with either, but neither seems to me a good tool, especially for a beginner. A regular blender can be used safely only for very small batches, and if overfilled may pop its lid and spew the soap mixture all over. Also, both these tools—especially the mixer—can beat in so much air that the soap texture is poor.

Checking the temperature seems such an easy way to tell if the soap mixture is ready to pour. Why don't all soapmaking books tell you to do that?

Because I worked it out myself while writing this one! I think it's a great technique, especially for beginners, because you don't have to depend entirely on your judgment.

In my tests, I could pour out a mixture after a temperature rise of two to three degrees Fahrenheit (one or two degrees Celsius) and get good soap even if I wasn't yet sure from visual signs that the mixture was ready. With a rise of ten degrees Fahrenheit (five or six degrees Celsius), the mixture was at heavy trace and in danger of solidifying in the pot! (Keep in mind that these specific temperature differences are for my own recipes and batch size as given in this book.)

In fairness to earlier authors, this method might work only when using a stick blender or other rapid mixer, which hasn't been common among craft soapmakers for that long. If you were hand stirring, I don't know if you could detect the rise, because you'd be generating heat more slowly and might be losing it about as fast. Also, a good digital thermometer helps a lot, and they've only recently become so affordable.

What is false trace? I read about that, and now I'm not sure if my soap has come to trace, or if it's just false trace.

"False trace" is when your soap mixture thickens considerably but then re-separates into lye solution and fat. It's rare, but it can sometimes happen when the temperature of your mixture falls below the recommended range, causing melted fat to start to resolidify. The thickening can fool you into thinking the mixture has saponified when it really hasn't.

With hand stirring, this cooling and thickening might happen anytime, but with a stick blender, you would probably only see it right after you start blending. You'll know it's too early for saponification to have more than barely begun, and in any case, the mixture will show no significant temperature rise. So, just keep blending, and the mixture should appear normal in a minute or so.

Why is your explanation of superfatting different from others I've read?

Superfatting is the term for including a buffer of extra fat in a recipe to make sure all lye is neutralized. Confusingly, some soapmakers instead use the term to mean adding part of the fat just before pouring the soap into the mold. This is done to save the most expensive "luxury" butters and oils till the lye has been neutralized by the other fat. This is supposed to let the late addition retain its distinctive, desirable qualities. Though the reasoning makes sense, some soapmakers believe this method has no benefit over adding all fats at once.

How do you make marbled soap?

Here's one way. Pour a little of the thickened soap mixture from the pot into a bowl. Add your colorant to the bowl and mix well. Now pour the colored mixture back into the pot and stir once or twice, just enough to swirl it around. Then pour the marbled soap mixture into the mold.

How do I make round soap?

Round soap can be made using plastic pipe as a mold. The main problem seems to be getting the soap out of the pipe. You can find various schemes on the Web for making and using such molds.

Do I really have to wait a couple of weeks to use my soap? Is there any way to speed that up?

If you're sure your soap mold can stand the heat, you can set it covered in a regular oven at around 170°F (77°C) right after you pour your soap into it. After two hours, turn off the oven without opening the door and let everything cool for several hours or overnight. The soap will be ready to use. When this heating technique is added to cold process soapmaking, the combined method is called *cold process oven process,* or CPOP (pronounced "SEE-pop").

Some woods used for molds will do fine in the oven, but others will blacken. Unfortunately, it's hard to predict ahead of time. Of course, you don't want to try this method with a milk carton.

What is rebatching, and what's it good for?

Rebatching is the reprocessing of a batch of soap to add ingredients. For instance, if your recipe was somehow off or you mismeasured, and you know exactly what was wrong, you could rebatch to correct the imbalance.

You can also rebatch to add special materials. These might include a luxury fat, or a scent that would have made the soap saponify too rapidly, or oatmeal, or a botanical such as lavender buds. Rebatching to add special ingredients is sometimes called *hand-milling*.

I don't have much experience in rebatching, but you can easily find information about it on the Web. Especially good for this is Kathy Miller's Web site, listed in the resources section of this book.

What does it mean when a scent is said to "accelerate trace"?

Some scents and other additives can make saponification happen so fast that the soap solidifies before you get a chance to pour it into your mold. "Accelerates trace" is the way manufacturers describe this potential problem. When the soap "seizes up" like that in the pot, it doesn't make the soap dangerous, just misshapen.

It's said that you can prevent the seizing by keeping the scent cool and adding it when the mixture just begins to thicken. Personally, I avoid such scents or else save them for rebatching.

I've read that a failed soap batch has to be disposed of as hazardous waste. Is that true?

I've read that too. The statement is puzzling because lye, the only hazardous component of soap, is routinely poured down drains to clean them. How could it be any more hazardous when partly used up in saponification?

A little research confirmed that, at least in my community, the mixture would not be considered hazardous waste. However, the fat in a soap mixture could clog your drain.

Why don't you describe the signs of a failed soap batch like other books do?

Frankly, I don't have much experience with soap failures. The few that I've had nearly all came when I was experimenting to see if I *could* make a recipe fail. The other one came when I tried an online calculator that wasn't set up correctly (and once I identified the error, I fixed that soap easily with rebatching). But I've *never* had soap fail when it was made from a properly designed recipe and with the methods I recommend.

As I said before, most failures seem to come from soapmakers trying to create their own recipes before they're ready. Others come from inadequate mixing when stirring by hand. After reading this book, you should be safeguarded from either source of problems.

Remember what my chemistry teacher friend told me: "If you just measure correctly, control the temperature, and mix your ingredients well, you'll get soap."

Why would that fail?

A Few Final Thoughts

To refine the instructions in this book, I've asked the opinions of many soapmakers and sifted the results. I've experimented with suggestions and modified my own procedures. I've tried to trim away unnecessary, cumbersome, or confusing directions.

The methods described here work for me and they work for my students. But not everyone will agree with all I've recommended—and that's to be expected. There's more than one good way to do almost anything in soapmaking.

Besides the techniques I've offered, I'd like to leave you with a few thoughts about basic approach.

• Never get lax in your safety measures, but don't be afraid of soapmaking, either.

• Wait to develop your own soap recipes till you've mastered the basis process of soapmaking.

• Question tradition—experiment.

Soapmaking is fun, creative, and rewarding. You'll be amazed at the beautiful soaps you make, at a cost far less than you'd pay if you bought them.

Enjoy soapmaking!

Resources

Author Online!

For updates and more resources,
visit Anne's Soapmaking Page at

www.annelwatson.com/soapmaking

Where to Learn More

Books

Here are the books I consider especially useful for beginners making cold process soap.

The Everything Soapmaking Book, by Alicia Grosso, Adams Media Corporation, Avon, Massachusetts, 2003. This is an excellent general source of soapmaking information. Unfortunately, it's out of print, so look for a used copy.

Essentially Soap, by Robert S. McDaniel, Krause Publications, Iola, Wisconsin, 2000. McDaniel is a chemist who makes soap and writes well. I would have thought a professional scientist's book would be out of reach for a beginner, but it's one of the clearest explanations of soapmaking I've read.

The Soapmaker's Companion, by Susan Miller Cavitch, Storey Publishing, North Adams, Massachusetts, 1997. A good reference, with detailed descriptions of the properties of various ingredients.

Web Sites

Anne's Soapmaking Page

Check here for the latest results of my experiments in soapmaking. There's always more to try and to learn!

www.annelwatson.com/soapmaking

SoapCalc

This site is one of the most useful sources of soapmaking information and formula analysis. It's nearly indispensable if you're designing your own recipes.

www.soapcalc.net

Miller's Homemade Soap Pages

Kathy Miller's Web site. Has soapmaking instructions and a page listing fats and their properties. An especially good resource for rebatching.

www.millersoap.com

Soap Nuts

A large library of resources from members of the Soapnuts Yahoo group.

www.soapnuts.com

Cole Brothers

Has soapmaking instructions and a page that lists fats and their properties.

www.colebrothers.com/soap

Soapmaking Dictionary

Defines dozens of terms used in soapmaking, courtesy of the Coconut Coast Handmade Soap Co.

www.ccnphawaii.com/glossary.htm

Skinesscentuals

Good basic information, especially about properties of fats.

home.earthlink.net/~skinesscentuals

Email Discussion Lists

There are many soapmaking lists, all with different personalities. Some encourage beginners and are excellent places for questions, while other lists are mainly for professionals. Some lists thrive on debate, while others forbid it. Search on the terms "soapmaking" and "soap making" at Yahoo Groups (groups.yahoo.com) and see what lists appeal to you. Then try a few and stick with what you like best.

Some lists sponsor cooperative buys of soapmaking supplies. These operations vary in quality. Probably the safest way to find a good co-op group is to get involved with a mailing list and then ask the other members for a referral.

Where to Get Supplies

In this list, suppliers in the western U.S. are ones I've used myself and can personally recommend. For most of the rest, I've relied on recommendations from experienced soapmakers who are acquainted with them.

United States

Bramble Berry

> 2138 Humboldt Street
> Bellingham, Washington 98225
> 877-627-7883
> 360-734-8278
> www.brambleberry.com

Majestic Mountain Sage

> 2490 South 1350 West
> Nibley, Utah 84321
> 435-755-0863
> www.thesage.com

Kangaroo Blue

23824 West Andrew Road, #103
Plainfield, Illinois 60585
630-999-8132
www.kangarooblue.com

Oregon Trail Soap Supplies & More

Evans Creek Road
Rogue River, Oregon 97537
541-582-8995
www.oregontrailsoaps.com

Wholesale Supplies Plus

10035 Broadview Road
Broadview Heights, Ohio 44147
800-359-0944
440-526-6556
www.wholesalesuppliesplus.com

Soapcrafters

Their supplies include pH strips.

6255 McLeod Drive, Suite 15
Las Vegas, Nevada 89120
877-484-5121
702-430-1745
www.soapcrafters.com

The Ponte Vedra Soap Shoppe

Tournament Plaza, 830-13 A1A North, #496
Ponte Vedra Beach, Florida 32082
904-543-8296
www.pvsoap.com

From Nature With Love

341 Christian Street
Oxford, Connecticut 06478
800-520-2060
203-702-2500
www.fromnaturewithlove.com

Candles and Woodcrafts

Their supplies include wooden soap molds.

Antoine, Arkansas 71922
870-379-2398
www.candlesandwoodcrafts.com

Snowdrift Farm

Their supplies include pH strips.

4420 North Highway Drive
Tucson, Arizona 85705
520-887-9431
www.snowdriftfarm.com

Soaper's Choice (Columbus Foods)

Specializes in soapmaking fats.

> 30 East Oakton Street
> Des Plaines, Illinois 60018
> 800-322-6457
> 773-265-6500
> www.soaperschoice.com

Old Will Knott Scales

Inexpensive scales that read in both ounces and grams.

> Professional Retail Service
> 10750 Irma Drive, Unit 4
> Northglenn, Colorado 80233
> 877-761-0322
> www.oldwillknottscales.com

Sciencc Kit Science Education Supplies

A source for pH strips.

> 777 East Park Drive
> P.O. Box 5003
> Tonawanda, New York 14150
> 800-828-7777
> www.sciencekit.com

Canada

Island Artisan Supply

Box 458
Merville, British Columbia V0R 2M0
250-218-1280
www.islandartisansupply.ca

Voyageur Soap & Candle Company

19257 Enterprise Way, Unit 14
Surrey, British Columbia V3S 6J8
800-758-7773
604-530-8979
www.soapandcandleco.com

Saffire Blue

538 Highway #3
Courtland, Ontario, N0J 1E0
877-248-1115
519-286-0295
www.saffireblue.ca

United Kingdom

G. Baldwin & Co.

171–173 Walworth Road
London SE17 1RW
(0)207 703 5550
www.baldwins.co.uk

Soap Basics

23 Southbrook Road
Melksham, Wiltshire SN12 8DS
(0)122 589 9286
www.soapbasics.co.uk

The Soap Kitchen

Hatchmoor Industrial Estate, Units 2D–E
Hatchmoor Road
Torrington, Devon EX38 7HP
(0)180 562 2944
www.thesoapkitchen.co.uk

The Soapmakers Store

Quatro Park, Unit 3
Blakelands Industrial Estate
Tanners Drive
Milton Keynes MK14 5FJ
(0)190 833 4108
www.soapmakers-store.com

Butterbur & Sage, Ltd.

3–5 Cremyll Road
Reading RG1 8NQ
(0)118 950 5100
www.butterburandsage.com

Australia

Aussie Soap Supplies

P.O. Box 165
Palmyra, Western Australia 6957
(08) 9339 1885
www.aussiesoapsupplies.com.au

Heirloom Body Care

78 Barnes Road
Llandilo, New South Wales 2747
(02) 4777 4457
www.heirloombodycare.com.au

Hawthorn Bay

Soap molds.

33 Anzac Crescent
Williamstown, Victoria 3016
(03) 9397 1460
www.hawbay.com.au

New Zealand

Aromatics & More

9J Trading Place
Henderson, West Auckland
(09) 835 4330
www.aromaticsandmore.com

Where to Find Design Tools

Online Calculators

SoapCalc

This is widely considered the finest soap design tool available, and it's free! Includes lye, water, INS values, and properties of fats.

> www.soapcalc.net

Bramble Berry Lye Calculator

> www.brambleberry.com/Pages/Lye-Calculator.aspx

Cranberry Lane's Lye Calculator

> www.cranberrylane.com/calculator.htm

Majestic Mountain Sage's Lye Calculator

> www.thesage.com/calcs/lyecalc2.php

Pine Meadows Lye Calculator

> www.pinemeadows.net/lyecalc.php

Computer Programs

SoapMaker

This program features a graphical display of soap hardness, fluffy lather, stable lather, and emollient properties of any given mixture of fats. It can calculate a recipe's percentages of individual fats from their quantities, and vice versa. It can also calculate the cost of supplies per bar, while the professional version keeps track of supply inventory.

www.soapmaker.ca

SoapCalc

This is a simple spreadsheet that can calculate lye and water, figure your cost per bar, and also re-size recipes for use in an ordinary blender. It doesn't have the fats properties information contained in SoapMaker. (This SoapCalc is not to be confused with the free SoapCalc you can use on the Web.)

www.colebrothers.com/soapcalc

Index

About the Author

Anne L. Watson made soap professionally under the company name Soap Tree before deciding that soapmaking was more fun as a hobby than as a business. In her other life, she is now retired from a long and honored career as a historic preservation architecture consultant.

Anne's other published books include *Milk Soapmaking, Smart Lotionmaking, Baking with Cookie Molds,* and several novels. Anne, her husband, Aaron, and their cat, Skeeter, live in Friday Harbor, Washington. You can visit her at

www.annelwatson.com

19193496R00063

Made in the USA
Lexington, KY
10 December 2012